WOMEN'S PRAYER SERVICES

Edited by Iben Gjerding
and Katherine Kinnamon

TWENTY-THIRD PUBLICATIONS
Mystic, Connecticut

Second Printing   February 1988

North American Edition 1987
Twenty-Third Publications
P.O. Box 180
Mystic CT 06355
(203) 536-2611

Originally published by World Council of Churches (Geneva, Switzerland) as *No Longer Strangers: A Resource for Women and Worship)*.

ISBN 0-89622-329-9
Library of Congress Catalog Card Number 86-51536

Contents

FOREWORD

For hundreds of years, Christians have attempted to name and describe the God of our faith, who, we have found, cannot be contained within the limitations of our human languages, a God who is so totally other, a God so unlike us in all ways. Yet, we have had to rely on our own experiences and relationships to convey who this God is. We have done so because while we believe our God to be a glorious God who cannot possibly begin to resemble our human condition, we also profess that we have been created in the image and likeness of our God. It is on this basis that we are able to talk of our relationship with the one who created and sustains us.

Most often, though, we have limited this image to a masculine one and today a response has come from both women and men who have begun to employ a God-language that includes feminine qualities as well as those that know no gender. And so, hundreds of years of prayer that has been permeated by a masculine perspective and language is beginning to be touched by a new sensitivity to the wider experience of humankind.

A Latin axiom, *lex orandi, lex credendi,* tells us that the way we pray is the way we believe. That is, the words and actions of our prayer experiences speak not only of our praise, thanksgiving, and petition to our God, but also of what we believe and hold to be true in the depths of our hearts. Our male-dominated worship has been reflective of who we have believed God to be. To hear God referred to as Mother and given feminine characteristics can be an especially uncomfortable situation for some who happen to find themselves in communities that make an effort to recognize the life experiences of *all* people of faith. Yet even more faithful have become uncomfortable with the inadequate and limited language that has come to us through tradition to describe our relationship with God.

Women's Prayer Services invites us to promote a new perspective wherever possible in our churches, a perspective that will only become acceptable as it comes to be used habitually in the years ahead. This book is a significant contribution to this effort. The editors affirm, "This book is one small offering toward the day when the worship life of our churches will reflect the experiences of the whole people of God, the day when we will be a community of women and men who lift their collective voices in praise to the glory of God."

This resource is a collection of the writings of women of various faith traditions from many regions of the world who have prayed from their own experience to a God who is a life-giving, nurturing God who comforts us as a mother cares for her children. It is a rich expression of the faith of women that will serve as a source for personal meditation and reflection, as well as a resource for communal prayer.

This book is a worship workbook, a working resource for worship. It offers a variety of components of prayer—calls to worship, litanies and readings, psalms, prayers, confessions of sins, benedictions, and reflections—that can be used to create worship experiences and provide inspiration for our own creativity. While these writings are primarily the work of women, they should not be limited in their use. All Christians who gather for prayer and take time for private reflection, whoever they may be, should be called beyond their present understanding of our Creator, for what is the purpose of our lives but to come to know in a very intimate way the God who cares for us? And how else do we come to know another than by discovering over time that individual's many facets and qualities?

May you and your worship community find in the pages of this book a rich witness of faith that unfolds for you yet another dimension of God who is Mother, Father, and creator of all!

Debra A. Hintz
Author of *Gathering Prayers*
and *Prayer Services for Parish Meetings*

CHAPTER ONE

INTRODUCING THE ISSUE

Hallelujah!
Praise God!
Praise God in the sanctuary
Praise God in the mighty firmament
Praise God with trumpet sound;
with flute and harp; with timbrel and dance;
with strings and pipe!
Praise God with sounding cymbals;
with loud clashing cymbals
Let everything that breathes praise God
Praise God! Hallelujah!   Psalm 150

The blessing of the God of Sarah and of Abraham,
the blessing of the Son, born of the virgin Mary,
the blessing of the Holy Spirit who broods over us
as a mother with her children,
be with you all. Amen.

These two passages illustrate the hope which lies behind the creation of this book. On the one hand we share the desire of all Christians to praise God—the creator, redeemer and sustainer of our lives—in everything we do. In Psalm 150, the psalmist tells us that our purpose is to worship God in the midst of our lives, with all that makes up our lives. As contemporary Christian women, we find comfort in the psalmist's words which speak of the breadth and height and diversity that is possible when we make our approach to the Divine.

"Let *everything* that breathes praise God!"

On the other hand, we share the desire of many women to see the Church's worship and praise reflect the experience of the *whole* Christian community: women as well as men.

"The God of Sarah *and* of Abraham"

The contemporary benediction quoted above helps to recall the crucial role women have had in the story of our faith. It is also a reminder to us that the experience of women can reveal important, and sometimes overlooked, dimensions of God's activity in the world.

"The blessing of the Holy Spirit who broods over us as a *mother* with her children."

Historically the experience and witness of women have not always been seen as a vital ingredient for the worship life of the Church. As a result, women and men have begun, in recent years, to raise questions about the nature and integrity of Christian worship—questions which call for a reassessment of our worship traditions. When a community gathers to praise God, they have asked, what perspective guides the shape of the worship experience? *Whose* experience does it reflect? What symbols and images are used in song, prayer and litany? Do they reflect the *whole* people of God, or just one segment? Does the worship of our traditions include women's experience? Is it reflective of the part women have had in biblical history and in the history of the Church? Isn't it possible to expand the language and symbols of our worship to include women, while remaining faithful to the message of the Gospel?

Within the last decade, a growing, worldwide community of women and men has begun to offer—in response to these questions—new worship expressions. They have turned to scripture and tradition, as well as to their lived experiences, for guidance. It is a spirit of renewal which they and we are seeking.

In response to the author of Psalm 150, we have carried the charge—that our worship reflect our lives—with us as we have gathered material for this worship workbook. Like the psalmist, we have been listening with all our senses to new voices of women who begun to put to word, dance, song and prayer their own faith witness.

How We Began

As women representing several different international Christian organizations in Geneva, we were looking for a way to consolidate and share the immense amount of new worship material we had in our respective files—material collected from local congregations and women's groups, at meetings, seminars, and ecumenical celebrations over the past few years. Most of these new worship resources were written by women—reflecting on their life experiences and the interaction between those experiences and their faith.

As our very informal plan for resource-sharing developed, we thought that such a collection might be useful for a wider audience as well—women and men who are discovering their right and ability, as Christians, to worship creatively. *Women's Prayer Services* is the result of this desire for a working resource for worship. We believe that the liturgical material we have chosen to include stands as a rich witness to the liberating power of the Gospel. It is a sharing of the ways women in their various contexts--alone and in community, in silence or in full voice—express their faith through worship.

What We Intend

Women's Prayer Services is not meant to be the final word on women and worship. It is not a history of liturgical changes in the Church. Nor is it a theological exposition about the nature of worship. It is a workbook, a tool. It is meant to encourage women and men to explore new forms of liturgy as a means of expressing their faith. With this book as a working guide, we hope that you will creatively explore new possibilities for worship, encouraged by the expressions of faith you find within these pages.

Finally, *Women's Prayer Services* is meant to be used as a source for personal meditations and reflection--a chance to find your own voice or dance or prayer, a chance to know the pain and joy of another's faith journey.

Our Criteria for Selecting Material

In moving beyond the idea of something for our own personal use to a resource book for a general audience, we had to decide what criteria we would use in selecting material from what was in our files. We know there are many other networks for finding new liturgical work by women, which are not represented here. As this is a "working" book, we hope you will search out these other resources, file them within the pages of this volume, and send us a copy.

An initial assumption was that the liturgical material included would be predominantly by women, representing a variety of worshipping traditions, cultures, and different regions of the world. We felt it imperative that all language in this book be non-sexist and inclusive in nature. Women are moving past the point in their spiritual lives when they can accept worship language and imagery which reflects an experience that excludes them.

We have also looked seriously at the language used today to address God. Can images of God be recovered—from scripture, tradition, experience—which are other than male images? Shouldn't we think of God as both tender and stern, loving and judging, masculine and feminine, thus stressing the wholeness of the Divine. As you read through the liturgical material we have chosen, it is clear that the answer to these questions is a resounding, "Yes!" Increasingly, women are finding within the traditions of their faith—or are creating for themselves—images of God which allow them to breathe and find space within the structures and symbols of the Church.

Finally we asked of the selections, "Are they authentic?" Whether prayer or song, call to worship or benediction, do they speak to us of women's life experiences and faith struggles? Again, we think the answer is a loud, "Hallelujah, yes!" They range from a litany about the history and power of women—giving us a structure for praising women in our various cultures—to a faith affirmation by a woman who sees God as her daily two hundred grams of gruel. These are our voices— praising God, confessing Christ, wherever we are in the world and in our faith journeys.

An Eschatological Note

With three or four exceptions, only women's worship expressions are reflected within these pages. Many centuries have passed in which the voice of women has been absent from the formulation and leadership of worship in our churches. This book is one small offering toward the day when the worship life in our churches will reflect the experiences of the whole people of God, the day when we will be a community of women and men who lift their collective voices in praise, to the glory of God.

CHAPTER TWO

SUGGESTIONS FOR CHANGE

The purpose of this chapter is to suggest several ways to approach the resource material which follows. We want to stress, however, that these are only suggestions; the most important thing is that this book be used as a tool. Explore and experiment with the material, but do not feel bound by any of our suggestions, or by any of the worship models presented.

The first suggestion is, quite simply, that this material be read for your own personal enjoyment and inspiration. These creative expressions should be seen as a way to understand, and to share in, the faith responses of women and men around the world. This understanding and sharing is perhaps at the heart of the workbook—the recognition of a rich and diversified witness to a common faith.

Second, on a more practical level, we hope that the resource material collected here will be used in public settings—conferences or services, women's meetings or prayer groups—any public forum where it is appropriate to provide meditative or worship material. The introduction and acceptance of inclusive language and images into our ecclesial vocabularies and symbol systems will happen only in so far as we promote this language by using it, whenever possible.

A third suggestion, following on the others, is that these resources be used in creating new worship expressions or in renewing the regular worship patterns of your congregation or community. The hesitation to make changes in worship forms is understandable considering the traditional patterns of church authority with which we have lived. Nevertheless, it is worth remembering that many "traditional" forms of worship are themselves the result of a spirit of renewal at some point in the history of the Church. Contemporary worship patterns, whether we view them positively or negatively, grew out of a new understanding of the relationship between God and the world. These patterns were seen as a means of transforming worship life. The problem is that what was innovative at one point in history may be seen and experienced today as a rigid tradition incapable of expanded meanings or symbols which would include women. The spirit or intention of renewal has been lost.

Until recently, laity—expecially women—have not had the opportunity for creative leadership within the areas of worship, liturgy or sacramental life. Certainly in terms of priestly functions, theology, the language and imagery of worship, women have been largely excluded. Increasingly, however, women are helping to renew and expand the worship life of the Church. With a variety of voices and messages, women are creating "new songs". Like those of Miriam and Mary, their "songs" are joyful, contemplative, angry, prayerful reflections of their lives and faith. *Women's Prayer Services* is a small sample of those reflections. We encourage you to use these resources in reshaping or supplementing traditional worship services or in creating new worship celebrations.

Finally, we want to suggest several ways in which you can experiment in making liturgical changes. Most of the suggestions are simple and straightforward. Nevertheless, they make a difference in the tone and spirit of a worship service. They may also help reveal what effects language and imagery have on our worship patterns.

- Try changing the words "Lord" and "He" to "God," whenever they appear in liturgical material.

- Use words that evoke new images of God. We have included a list of twenty-five names for God. Some may seem awkward at first, but we must try to institute new images if we are to break the pattern of male-dominated God-language. Again, these are only suggestions. We encourage you to find your own images and words for our Heavenly Creator, our Companion and our Delight.

The Source (of all that is)	Presence [1]
Lady of peace	Power
Lady of wisdom	Light
Lady of love	Strength
Lady of birth	Mourner
Lord of stars	Essence
Lord of planets	Renewer
Consoler	Comforter
Mother	Simplicity
Home	Giver and Taker
Maker (of all)	Friend
Companion	
Keeper	
Healer	
Bakerwoman	

[1] *The names in the second column of this list come from the book "Image-Breaking/Image-Building," L. Clark, E. Walker and M. Ronan, Pilgrim Press 1979, page 68f. The first column of names come from the liturgical pieces we have included in chapter three.*

- Replace masculine expressions in the well-known hymns of your traditions, with more inclusive language. For example, in the recently published songbook, *Because We Are One People*,[2] the English carol "God Rest Ye Merry Gentlemen," has been retitled, "God Rest Ye Joyful People All."
  Rewriting songs is a talent many of us do not feel we have. But there are simple things we can do. In songs with words like "sons," "man," or "men," which refer to people in general, we can substitute words like "child," "folk," or "children." An enormous number of new hymns and songs—many of them by women—have been written within the last ten years. Most of them stress inclusive language and message. We invite you to consult our bibliography for a short list of song-books now available and which we feel have taken seriously the challenge for inclusive language songs.

- Rewrite traditional prayers, taking out exclusive language while being careful to remain faithful to the intent of the prayer.

- Taking note of the examples included in our resource material, write your own psalms or prayers. Use the Old Testament psalms as a guide to structure if you wish, but let your words of praise and supplication be a reflection of your own situation, or that of your community.

- When choosing biblical texts for personal or public use, choose texts which reflect on the situation of women or which reflect feminine images of God. This underlines the fact that God can be described as both female and male; that, in fact, God is neither male nor female, but rather is beyond human categories.

> *Examples: Genesis 1:27,*
> *Numbers 11:12,*
> *Deuteronomy 32:18,*
> *Nehemiah 9:21,*
> *Job 38:29,*
> *Psalms 22:9, 90:2, 147:3.*
> *Isaiah 1:2, 42:14, 49:15, 66:13,*
> *Hosea 11:3-4,*
> *Matthew 23:37,*
> *Luke 15:8-10.*

---

[2] Because We Are One People. *Ed., Ruth C. Duck, The Ecumenical Women's Center, Chicago 1974, page 47.*

In many instances two biblical texts have the same intent, but the main character or image is male in one, and female in the other. For example, instead of the well-known story of the leper (Luke 5:12-16), use the story of the woman with the hemorrhage (Luke 8:43-48). Other parallel passages include the parables of the lost sheep and the lost coin. Both proclaim God's love for the lost, but the second story speaks of God's love in the image of a housewife.

You can also choose biblical texts about the role of women in society as a way to show their history in the Bible. The part women had in ancient biblical times is often ignored or diminished. It is possible to be faithful to the Gospel but also to enrich the reading of scripture by giving more prominence to texts which put women in the center of action and reflection.

Examples: Genesis 16, 27:5-17,
Exodus 1:15-21, 15:20-21,
Joshua 2:2-22,
Judges 4:4-24, 5:6-18, 24-31,
1 Kings 21:1-16,
2 Kings 4:8-37,
Matthew 15:21-28, 25:1-13,
Luke 1:26-55, 4:38-39, 7:36-50, 8:1-3, 8:40-56,
10:38-42, 13:10-17, 13:20-21, 18:1-8, 21:1-4,
23:27-31, 23:49, 55-56, 24:1-11,
John 4:3-42, 8:3-11, 11:20-27, 19:25, 20:1-2,
11-18,
Acts 9:36-42, 10:13-15, 40.

● A final suggestion for making changes is to experiment with the sermon format. We have included some examples of what women have been doing in a number of different settings. (See section ten of chapter three.)

A General Outline of a Worship Service

The resource material in the following chapter, as well as many of the suggestions and observations just made, can be useful in the renewal of established worship patterns and in the creation of new worship formats. Chapter three is divided according to major parts of worship services found in most of our churches. Unfortunately, in the space of this short volume, it is impossible to represent adequately the variety of worshipping traditions. Nevertheless, the description below may prove useful as a way to see how these parts of worship are generally understood. It is important to note that the service outlined here does not include a eucharistic liturgy.

Very simply, a worship service is an encounter with the Divine in community. From this premise, the logic of worship unfolds. Generally speaking, the beginning or entrance into worship is marked by the community with an affirmation of the presence of God in its midst. Frequently, there is also a statement concerning why the community has gathered before God. The divine presence compels us to acknowledge our shortcomings, to seek God's forgiveness and to give thanks for God's grace. In the knowledge of that forgiveness, the worshipping community then lays its requests before God in a sequence of prayers.

Worship proceeds with the hearing of God's response through scripture, the affirmation of faith and a sermon. The sermon tries to explicate the scripture reading and to point to its meaning for the lives of those present. Finally, there is "the sending forth into the world." The worshipping community is charged to look beyond the specific time spent in worship to its life in the larger community. This blessing, or benediction, promises the community that it will continue to enjoy God's presence in the time ahead. It serves to mark the end of worship and the community's departure from one another.

Some of these parts may be missing, or others added, in a worship service. This, however, is the general pattern. There is a need to hear and say certain things before God and in the midst of a witnessing community.

In summary, through song, prayer, proclamation, confession and forgiveness, the sequence of the service assists the participants:

● to recall and reflect on the saving acts of God recorded in scripture;

● to find and celebrate the presence of God in everyday life;

● to lay before God their deepest fears, joys and hopes;

● to dare acknowledge the holy within their lives and within the ordinary things of daily experience;

● to find hope through the goodness of God within their personal and communal lives;

● to give thanks for God's gracious love, expressed through Jesus Christ.

There are any number of texts on the nature of worship and liturgy which will explain practically and theologically what happens in a worship setting. What is offered here is not a theological explanation of worship but a description, in broad strokes, of the *flow* of worship. There is more that can, and probably should, be said about the how-to's of worship but we invite you to move on to the resource material. Let the women's voices represented there engage you, speak to you, teach you. Let them "sing" to you "a new song."

CHAPTER THREE

RESOURCES FOR WORSHIP

Come, let us Celebrate Together

Sisters and Brothers — Arise

Sisters and Brothers — Arise.
Arise and lift your hearts
Arise and lift your eyes
Arise and lift your voices.

The living God,
The living, moving Spirit of God
has called us together —
in witness
in celebration
in struggle.

Reach out toward each other.
Our God reaches out toward us!
Let us worship God!

Elizabeth Rice, USA

Song of Communion

Let's go to the corn patch
to the supper of the Lord
Jesus Christ is inviting
to his harvest of love
the cornfields shine
in the sunlight
let's go to the supper
of communion.

*From The Nicaraguan Campesino Mass
by Carlos Jejia Godoy and
Pablo Martinez, NICARAGUA*

❖

Three Questions[1]

Why have we gathered here?
We have responded to the gospel of God's love for us
in Jesus Christ.

What do we hope to do here?
We hope to be united with the faithful of all ages,
tongues, and races in praising the God of love and
power.

With what mission will we be sent from this place?
To be God's helpers in serving humanity, to spread
the gospel, and to resist the powers of evil.

All: Let us then draw near to God, who promises to forgive
us, to fill us with courage, and to be present with
us in this world and in the world to come. Amen.

Ruth C. Duck, USA

---

[1] *The pieces which are printed with two different type-sets are to be read in two
parts. This may be two persons, a liturgist and congregation, the congregation
divided into two groups, or other possibilities of your own creation.*

Come, Let Us Celebrate

Come,
Let us celebrate the supper of the Lord.
Let us make a huge loaf of bread
and let us bring abundant wine
like at the wedding of Cana.

Let the women not forget the salt.
Let the men bring along the yeast.
All: Let many guests come,
the lame, the blind, the crippled, the poor.

Come quickly.
Let us follow the recipe of the Lord.
All of us, let us knead the dough together
with our hands.
All: Let us see with joy
how the bread grows.

Because today
we celebrate
the meeting with the Lord.
Today we renew our commitment
to the Kingdom.
All: Nobody will stay hungry.

Elsa Tamez, MEXICO

2

Teach us to Know and Love you

A Litany of New Birth

O gracious God of life and birth,
How you labor, how you suffer, to bring forth the new creation!
Indeed, you cry out like a woman in childbirth.
And the Spirit groans with you.
But your cries become cries of joy,
As you behold fragile new life there before you.
All creation waits on tiptoe for the revealing of your daughters and sons;
We ourselves long to take part in the glorious liberty of your children.
Who can separate us from the love of God?
Even a mother might forget us,
Yet you will not forsake us!
O God, our God, how wonderful is your name in all the earth!

Ruth C. Duck, USA

Blessing the Bread — A Litany

Voice 1 In the beginning was God
2 In the beginning, the source of all that is
3 In the beginning, God yearning
4 God, moaning
1 God, labouring
2 God, giving birth
3 God, rejoicing
4 And God loved what she had made
1 And God said, "It is good".

Voice 2 Then God, knowing that all that is good is shared
3 held the earth tenderly in her arms
4 God yearned for relationship
1 God longed to share the good earth
2 And humanity was born in the yearning of God
3 We were born to share the earth

Voice 4 In the earth was the seed
1 In the seed was the grain
2 In the grain was the harvest
3 In the harvest was the bread
4 In the bread was the power

Voice 1 And God said, *All shall eat of the earth*
2 *All shall eat of the seed*
3 *All shall eat of the grain*
4 *All shall eat of the harvest*
1 *All shall eat of the bread*
2 *All shall eat of the power*

Voice 3 God said, *You are my people,*
4 *My friends,*
1 *My lovers,*
2 *My sisters,*
3 *And brothers*
4 *All of you shall eat*
1 *of the bread*
2 *And the power*
3 *All shall eat.*

Voice 4 Then God, gathering up her courage in love, said,
1 *Let there be bread!*
2 And God's sisters, her friends and lovers, knelt on the earth
3 planted the seeds
4 prayed for the rain
1 sang for the grain
2 made the harvest
3 cracked the wheat
4 pounded the corn
1 kneaded the dough
2 kindled the fire
3 filled the air with the smell of fresh bread
4 And there was bread!
1 And it was good!

Voice 2 We, the sisters of God, say today,
3 All shall eat of the bread,
4 And the power,
1 We say today,
2 All shall have power
3 And Bread.
4 Today we say,
1 Let there be bread.
2 And let there be power!
3 Let us eat of the bread and the power!
4 And all will be filled
1 For the bread is rising!

Voice 2 By the power of God
3 Women are blessed
2 By the women of God
3 The bread is blessed
4 By the bread of God
1 The power is blessed
4 By the power of bread
1 The power of women
2 The power of God
3 The people are blessed

1, 2, 3, 4 *The earth is blessed*

All And the bread is rising

Carter Heyward, USA

We Thank You, O God

For your love, which became flesh and lived among us in the person of Jesus Christ,

WE THANK YOU, O GOD.

For the lessons of love Christ taught us as he lived among women and men,

WE THANK YOU, O GOD.

Let us learn from Christ's example and begin to treat each other with love and respect,

WE EARNESTLY ASK YOUR HELP, O GOD.

For Christ's example, which showed us that Mary's desire to learn was as worthy and important as Martha's desire to serve,

WE THANK YOU, O GOD.

For the healing ministry of Christ, which affirmed the faith of the women who touched the hem of his robe,

WE THANK YOU, O GOD.

For Christ's challenge to the woman at the well, which made her whole again and motivated her to evangelize her village,

WE THANK YOU, O GOD.

All: Christ has shown us that he knew women were important and should be loved and respected as God's daughters. Help us to love and respect all women and men and to remember that Christ's love was so strong that he was willing to die for our lack of love. May we be raised up as new creatures in Christ, freed of the lessons of prejudice and hatred that have been so carefully taught to us. Amen.

Willa Roghalr, USA

Kyrie

Christ, Christ Jesus
 Be one with us
Lord, Lord my God
 Be one with us
Christ, Christ Jesus
 Be in solidarity
Not with the oppressor class
which wrings out and devours
the community

But with the oppressed
with my people
which is thirsty for peace.

From The Nicaraguan Campesino Mass by Carlos Jejia Godoy and Pablo Martinez, NICARAGUA

A Litany of Women's Power

All: Spirit of Life, we remember today the women, named and unnamed, who throughout time have used the power and gifts you gave them to change the world. We call upon these foremothers to help us discover within ourselves your power—and the ways to use it to bring about the Kingdom of Justice and Peace.

We remember SARAH who with Abraham answered God's call to forsake her homeland and put their faith in a covenant with the Lord.
We pray for her power of faith.

We remember ESTHER and DEBORAH, who by acts of individual courage saved their nation.
We pray for their power of courage to act for the greater good.

We remember MARY MAGDALENE, and the other women who followed Jesus who were not believed when they announced the resurrection.
We pray for their power of belief in the face of skepticism.

We remember PHOEBE, PRISCILLA, and the other women leaders of the early church.
We pray for their power to spread the Gospel and inspire congregations.

We remember the Abbesses of the Middle Ages who kept faith and knowledge alive.
We pray for their power of leadership.

We remember TERESA of Avila and CATHERINE of Siena who challenged the corruption of the Church during the Renaissance.
We pray for their powers of intelligence and outspokenness.[2]

All: We remember our own mothers and grandmothers whose lives shaped ours.
We pray for the special power they attempted to pass on to us.

We pray for the women who are victims of violence in their homes.
May they be granted the power to overcome fear and seek solutions.
We pray for those women who face a life of poverty and malnutrition.
May they be granted the power of hopefulness to work together for a better life.

---

[2] *At this point you may wish to remember contemporary women, and their contributions, from your culture. Ex.: first woman ordained, first woman physician etc.*

We pray for the women today who are "firsts" in their fields. May they be granted the power to persevere and open up new possibilities for all women.

All: We pray for our daughters and granddaughters.
May they be granted the power to seek that life which is uniquely theirs.

(HERE, add any women you would like to remember or for whom you wish to pray)

All: We have celebrated the power of many women past and present. It is time now to celebrate ourselves. Within each of us is that same life and light and love. Within each of us lie the seeds of power and glory. Our bodies can touch with love; our hearts can heal; our minds can seek out faith and truth and justice. Spirit of Life, be with us in our quest. Amen.

Ann M. Heidkamp, USA

Teach Us to Know and Love You

O God of a thousand names and faces
Mother and father of all life on earth,
You who live in the cells of all life,
   Teach us to know and love you.

Lady of peace, of love, of wisdom,
Lord of all the stars and planets,
Best consoler, inward guest,
   Teach us to know and love you.

Giver of gifts and light of our hearts,
Fill the inmost depths of our hearts,
   And teach us to know and love you.

Wash what is soiled, heal what is wounded,
Bend what is rigid, warm what is frigid,
   And teach us to know and love you.

Restore to us our humanness,
   And teach us to know and love you.

Sharon Owens, USA

Let Us Love One Another

Dear friends, let us love one another, for love
comes straight from God.
**For those who love are God's children and
know God.**

God's love was manifested among us when God
sent Jesus into the world so that we might discover the
meaning of life through Christ.
**God's love is primary. All love flows from
the truth of God's love in Christ. This love has the
power to bring forgiveness to us all.**

Friends, if this is how God loved us, then we
should love one another in the same way.
**No one has ever seen God, but if we love
one another, God lives in us
and Christ's love is made
perfect in us.**

God is love; those who live in love live in God and
God lives in them.
**Thus we have courage as we face the judgment,
because our life in this world is strengthened by Christ.**

There is no fear in love; perfect love drives out all
fear. Fear is brought about by punishment, but if we are
perfected in love, we no longer worry about punishment.
We love because God first loved us.

If anyone says, "I love God," but hates sister or
brother, that person is a liar.
**If we do not love our sister or brother
whom we see, we cannot love God whom we do not see.
This, then, is the commandment Christ gave us: We who
love God must love our sisters and brothers too.**

1 John 4: 7-12, 16-21

3

In the Hour of Darkness, Hear my Voice

Oh God! What Hast Thou To Say?

What hast thou to say, O God?
Tell us, Lord, what's in thy mind?

Ten decades of life for tea we have given
    Ten more decades we now pour out;
All these years for our rights we have striven,
    But all our toil has brought us nought.
    For all this, what say'st thou?
    Tell us, Lord, what is thy thought?

As imported goods we were brought to these shores,
    As worthless goods we're now returned;
But for this land's wealth sweat poured from our pores,
    Now without rights in camps we herd.
    Seeing this, what say'st thou, God?
    Tell us then who are thine own?

They promised new life to entice us out,
    But all we saw were cemeteries;
All our hope was gone, saved money ran out,
    And lives became futilities.
    Now what hast thou to say, O God?
    Tell us, O Lord, what thou hast planned!

P. Mookan, Sri Lanka

27

I cry in the Night from the Torture Chamber

Psalm 130

From the depths, I cry to you oh Lord!
I cry in the night from the prison cell
and from the concentration camp
From the torture chamber
in the hour of darkness
hear my voice

     my S.O.S.

If you were to keep a record of sins
Lord, who would be blameless?
But you do pardon sins
you are not implacable as they are in their investigation!

I trust in the Lord and not in leaders
Nor in slogans
I trust in the Lord and not in their radios!

My soul hopes in the Lord
more than the sentinels of dawn
more than the way one counts the hours of night in a prison cell.

While we are imprisoned, they are enjoying themselves!
But the Lord is liberation
the freedom of Israel.

Clamo En La Noche
En La Camara De Tortura
by Ernesto Cardenal, NICARAGUA

28

4

Many Faces
I have Thought
Were you

Anoint Us

Spirit of God — Holy God, Wind of God,
Fire of God, Life of God...

Anoint us to be a people of your Good News,
yoked to break yokes,
sighted to bring sight, healed to be healers,
struggling to bring release.

Shower us and comfort us in the shining light
and darkness of your glorious mystery.
We invoke your mystery, not ours.
We invoke your clarity, not ours.
We invoke your truth, not ours.

Spirit of God — Holy God, Wind of God,
Fire of God, Life of God —
you who made Deborah and Miriam,
Mary and Dorcas, Joan of Arc,
Sojourner Truth and Rosa Parks[3]
cry out through the cosmos, cry out through us.
Make your justice, your work,
and your love real through our lives.
Amen.

Elizabeth Rice, USA

---

[3] *Sojourner Truth and Rosa Parks were early figures in struggles for human justice in the United States. You may wish to replace these names with names of women from your own context.*

Many Faces I Have Thought Were You

Many faces I have thought were you..
  The judging father
    successful demanding
      expecting excellence
    asking that I earn approval
     that I deserve attention
        ....hoping for his love.

Many faces I have thought were you..
  The caring mother
    martyred and all giving
      self sacrificing
    always thinking of others
     her way the only way
        ....longing for her love.

Many faces I have thought were you..
  A comforting friend
    to be depended on
     nurturer and guide
    with me in the desert
    walking through the valleys
     and long forgotten paths
       ....seeking love together.

Many faces I have thought were you..
  The giver of life and law
    all knowing
      all being
        all creating
    all seeing
     ever watchful
      even in the darkness of the night.
        ....afraid of your love.

Many faces I have thought were you..
  The tragic human figure
    loving .. hurting
      angry .. sad
  not spared the death of a son
    but one with us in suffering
        ....needing to be loved.

Many faces I have thought were you
  all of them .. and none.

Mary Ellen Gaylord, USA

For All People

Living God,
We pray for all people:
For those women shut off from a full
  life by tradition and practice.
For those people who are oppressed and
  exploited.
For those denied their freedom and
  dignity by systems and authorities.
For those forced to leave their home-
  lands because of their ideologies.
For those seeking answers and meaning
  to their lives within their own
  cultures and religions.
For those who labour too long and too
  hard only to barely feed and clothe
  themselves and their families.
For those forced to sell their bodies
  to survive
For those women and men who live lives
  of quiet desperation at the hands of
  the powerful and prestigious.
For these and all who suffer
We pray,
Asking that the Church may once again
Give joyful expression to your
  creative love
Which breaks down barriers
  and unites person to person, woman to
  man, and community to community.
Which gives meaning and hope to empty
  lives
And makes us reach out to each other
  in generous self-giving.
Which makes us more complete ourselves.

So God,
Fulfill your promise in us
For the sake of all human beings
  through Jesus Christ.

ASIA

Let Me Pass the Day in Peace

O God, you have let me pass the day in peace,
Let me pass the night in peace,
O Lord, you have no Lord.
There is no strength but in you.
There is no unity but in your house.
Under your hand I pass the night.
You are my mother and my father.
You are my home. Amen.

From The Boran of Kenya

❖

The Intruders

Lord, we feel just like the sinner in the elegant house of Simon the Pharisee. We see ourselves as intruders, interrupting, out of place, causing confusion in the world of men and in their church. But we love you, Lord Jesus, you who saw the woman and who see us, you who love us and lift us up. You allow us to come to you with our defeats and sins, our tears and our kisses, with our wash-tubs and floor-rags, our diapers and scrubbrushes, with our feelings and our everyday concerns, our longings and expectations, and also with our knowledge and education, our new assignments and new responsibilities in society. We are sinners who ask for your forgiveness, but we are also strong, independent and unbeatable when we let you lift us up through your love. That is why we can go in peace and serve you with joy, wherever you lead us, as we go forth in prayer.

Brita Salomon, SWEDEN

❖

Prayer of St Anselm

And Thou, Jesus, sweet Lord,
Art Thou not also a mother?
Truly, Thou art a mother,
The mother of all mothers,
Who tasted death,
In Thy desire to give life to Thy children.

11th Century

By His Wounds You Have Been Healed

1 Peter 2:24

O God,
through the image of a woman[4]
crucified on the cross
I understand at last.

For over half of my life
I have been ashamed
of the scars I bear.
These scars tell an ugly story,
a common story,
about a girl who is the victim
when a man acts out his fantasies.

In the warmth, peace and sunlight of your presence
I was able to uncurl the tightly clenched fists.
For the first time
I felt your suffering presence with me
in that event.
I have known you as a vulnerable baby,
as a brother, and as a father.
Now I know you as a woman.
You were there with me
as the violated girl
caught in helpless suffering.

The chains of shame and fear
no longer bind my heart and body.
A slow fire of compassion and forgiveness
is kindled.
My tears fall now
for man as well as woman.

You, God,
can make our violated bodies
vessels of love and comfort
to such a desperate man.
I am honoured
to carry this womanly power
within my.body and soul.

You were not ashamed of your wounds.
You showed them to Thomas
as marks of your ordeal and death.
I will no longer hide these wounds of mine.
I will bear them gracefully.
They tell a resurrection story.   *CANADA*

---

[4] *In a Toronto church the figure of a woman, arms outstretched as if crucified, was hung below the cross in the chancel.*

On the Night Before He Died
Eucharistic Prayer

We give thanks to you, O God, for the goodness and love which you have made known to us in creation; in the calling of Israel to be your people; in your Word spoken through the prophets; and above all in the Word made flesh, Jesus your Christ: Whom you have sent, in these last days to be incarnate from Mary, our sister, to be the saviour and redeemer of the world; in whom you have delivered us from evil and made us worthy to stand before you; in whom you have brought us out of error into truth, out of sin into righteousness, out of death into life.

On the night before He died for us, our Saviour Jesus Christ took bread, and when He had given thanks to you, He broke it, and gave it to his disciples, and said, "Take, eat: This is my Body, which is given for you. Do this for the remembrance of me."

After supper He took the cup of wine; and when He had given thanks, He gave it to them, and said, "Drink this, all of you; this is my Blood of the new Covenant, which is shed for you and for many for the forgiveness of sins. Whenever you drink it, do this for the remembrance of me."

Therefore, according to his command, O gracious God,

We remember his death. We proclaim his resurrection. We await his coming in glory. And we offer our sacrifice of praise and thanksgiving to you, Maker of all; presenting to you, from your creation, this bread and this wine.

We pray you, gracious God, to send your Holy Spirit upon these gifts that they may be the sacrament of the Body of Christ, the Blood of the new Covenant. Unite us to Jesus, our brother, in his sacrifice, that we too may be acceptable, being sanctified by the Holy Spirit. In the fullness of time, bring all things into your Christ's rule, and bring us, together with (and) all your saints, into the everlasting heritage of your sons and daughters; through Jesus Christ, our Saviour, the first-born of all creation, the head of the Church, and the author of our salvation.

By whom, and with whom, and in whom, in the unity of the Holy Spirit, all honour and glory is yours, most Holy One, now and forever.

Amen.

Extract from
Mother Thunder Liturgy, USA

Lord, Remind Me

**Lord,
remind me when
I need to know,
you did not
ask me to
defend your Church
but to lay
down my life
for people.**

Bishop Colin O'Brien Winter
NAMIBIA

Our Hearts are often Fearful

But We Turn Away

All: Keeper and Companion of us all, forgive us.
You call us, like Eve, to co-create new worlds;
But we turn away and backslide into the comfortable
or the certain.
You call us, like Miriam, to march for freedom;
But we turn away and glory in how far we have
come, forgetting how far we have to go.
You call us, like Deborah, to judge our world,
to make decisions, and offer counsel;
But we turn away and apologize for our anger
and compromise our positions.
You call us, like Huldah, to do justice and love mercy;
But we turn away and practice our passivity,
purity, and piety in domestic spheres.
You call us, like Naomi and Ruth, to love one another;
But we turn away and compete, taking vengeance
on those most like ourselves.
You call us, like Mary, to be faithful bearers of your word;
But we turn away and strive to become perfectionists.
You call us, like Thecla and Phoebe, to begin a new church;
But we turn away and accept a place in the system,
rationalizing things the way they are.
All: Merciful Healer, we do not claim our gifts.
We do not face up to your call. We do not
appreciate your partnership in creating a new
community and a new world. Today we repent.
We turn from our old ways and commit ourselves
to new partnerships for holding on and to new
visions for a different heaven and earth.

From
Liturgy of Hope
from The Study on "The Community of
Women and Men in the Church",
and Commission on Faith
and Order, NCCC, USA

How Can We Sing Your Song in a Strange Land?

Who are we, God, that we should confess you?
We can hardly speak for ourselves;
how could we speak in your name?
We believe in your Word,
but our minds are often full of doubt.
We trust your promises,
but our hearts are often fearful.
We remember that we have been baptized,
but we often forget to respond to your grace.
Captivate our minds, God,
and let your Spirit dwell in our hearts
that we may know the love
which you have given to us in your Son.

God, we believe — forgive our unbelief.

How can we call new disciples for you, God,
While our community, your church, is divided
and all too conformed to the pattern of this world?
We preach your power of love
while we succumb, like all others,
to the love of power.
We proclaim your justice
while we remain caught up in the structures
of injustice.
Awaken in us the spirit of unity
that we may feel the pain of your body divided,
and yearn and reach out for fuller union with you
and with one another.
Inflame us with the power of your love
that it may consume the vanity of power.
Make us hunger and thirst for justice,
that our words may be given authority
as signs of your justice.

God, we believe — forgive our unbelief.

How can we sing your song, O God
in a strange land?
How can we witness to your all-embracing love
with lives full of painful contradictions?
How can we be ambassadors of reconciliation
in a world enslaved by sin and death,
where children suffer and starve,
and many labor in vain
while a few live in luxury;
where, in midst of our lives,
we dwell under the shadow of death?

What answer shall we give to the suffering
(what shall we say in our own hearts)
when they cry from the depths:
''Where now is your God?''

God, we believe — forgive our unbelief.

God, mysterious and hidden,
it is in our captivity that you reveal yourself
as the open door,
it is in the midst of our pain
that your suffering love heals us,
and it is in the depths of our despair
that you shine upon us
as the morning star of hope.
God crucified, God risen:
come, transform the necessities
that are laid upon us
into freedom, joy and praise everlasting.

God, we believe — forgive our unbelief!

All: God, we believe — help our unbelief!

*From
The Worship Book
of the 5th Assembly
of the WCC, NAIROBI 1975*

Accept Our Deep Longing To Live

Oh God, our Father and Mother.
We confess today that Your own sons and daughters
in Christ have let you down.
Dominated by our fears, we have trampled and
smothered one another.
We have smothered the tenderness of man and the
creative thinking of woman.
Help women to discover honest and life-giving sisterhood.
Help men to open their hearts to each other in true brotherhood.
Help us to create a community of brothers and sisters
where we can live with each other in creative community
man with man, woman with woman, man with woman.

Your own church has often prevented people from seeing
Your fullness.
Help us not to flinch from the testimony of history,
religious wars, witchtrials, oppression of women.
Give us the courage to acknowledge honestly how Your name has been
used to justify detestable actions.
Your own children of faith bear guilt that burns.
Bring us to our senses and give us faith that renewal
and conversion is possible.

Jesus Christ, our brother.
We are seeking the secret of Your life, Your death and resurrection.
We rejoice in Your closeness to women and children,
to all that is regarded as weak and contemptible.

For the sake of love
You shared our loneliness, our conflicts with family and friends,
our pain when rejected and hurt.
Accept our deep longing to live the true life in You.
Help us to be free and open.
Help us to feel your closeness burning in our hearts
in spite of the jungle of theological interpretations and distortions.

Help us to share with each other our pain and joy,
our fears and hope.
Save us from chilliness and distance,
from teaching without life,
from seeking prestige and struggling for power.

We pray for those who hesitate to confess your name
You know them and their secret longing.
Do not let your sinful church and its fearful followers
hinder them in their seeking for you.

Kerstin Lindqvist
and Ulla Bardh, SWEDEN

6

A Witness to Christ's Rising was my Mother

As Smoke Is Blown Away

As smoke is blown away
and wax melts in the fire,
racism and oppression
disappear before the face of God.
The oppressed and trampled down
are set free in God's presence.
They rejoice and shout with joy.

Zephania Kameeta, NAMIBIA

I Believe

I believe in God, Mother-Father spirit
who called the world into being,
who created men and women and set them free to live in love,
in obedience and community.

I believe in God, who because of love for her creation,
entered the world to share our humanity,
to rejoice and to despair,
to set before us the paths of life and death;
to be rejected, to die, but finally
to conquer death and to bind the world to herself.

I believe in God who invites us into the community of the church
that we may, through faith and communion,
experience God's uplifting and sustaining grace;
that we may fulfil our human responsibility
and reach out for our neighbour;
that we may work to bring healing and wholeness
to a ruptured and uncertain world... and that we
may rejoice in the constancy of nature and the joy of life itself.

I believe in God whose word teaches us that the wheat and the tares
grow together; that the paths of life and death, good and evil,
too often converge... choices are not clearly defined...
but we confidently and responsibly tread the path we choose
and only God can be our judge.

I believe in God who is present and working in this world
through men and women.

I sense God's purpose in a spark of light here and there as
humankind struggles to keep a human face.
I know God's purpose as I watch children at play... hope
born anew in each generation... perhaps to be quickly extinguished,
perhaps to continue to burn brightly.

But for that hope I give thanks.

Norma, AUSTRALIA

A Wandering Aramean Was My Mother

A wandering Aramean was my mother
In Egypt she bore slaves.
Then she called to the God of our mothers.
Sarah, Hagar, Rebeccah, Rachel, Leah,
Praise God who hears, forever.

A warrior, judge, and harlot was my mother.
God used her from time to time.
She gave what she gave, and was willing.
Rahab, Jael, Deborah, Judith,
Praise God who takes, forever.

A Galilean virgin was my mother.
She bore our Life and Hope.
And a sword pierced her own soul, also.
Mary, bless'd among women, mother of God,
Praise God who loves, forever.

A witness to Christ's rising was my mother.
What angels said, she told.
The apostles thought it was an idle tale.
Mary, Mary Magdalene, Joanna, women, with them,
Praise God who lives, forever.

A faithful Christian woman was my mother.
A mystic, Martyr, Saint.
May we, with her, in every generation
Julian, Perpetua, Clare, Hilda,
Praise God who made us
     God who saved us
     God who keeps us all, forever.

Mother Thunder Mission, USA

Woman's Creed

I believe in God
who created woman and man in God's
own image
who created the world
and gave both sexes
the care of the earth.

I believe in Jesus
child of God
chosen of God
born of the woman Mary
who listened to women and liked them
who stayed in their homes
who discussed the Kingdom with them
who was followed and financed
by women disciples.

I believe in Jesus
who discussed theology with a woman
at a well
and first confided in her
his messiahship
who motivated her to go and tell
her great news to the city.

I believe in Jesus who received anointing
from a woman at Simon's house
who rebuked the men guests who scorned
her
I believe in Jesus
who said this woman will be remembered
for what she did —
minister for Jesus.

I believe in Jesus who healed
a woman on the sabbath
and made her straight
because she was
a human being.

I believe in Jesus
who spoke of God
as a woman seeking the lost coin
as a woman who swept
seeking the lost.

I believe in Jesus
who thought of pregnancy and birth
with reverence
not as punishment — but
as wrenching event
a metaphor for transformation
born again
anguish-into-joy.

I believe in Jesus
who spoke of himself
as a mother hen
who would gather her chicks
under her wing.

I believe in Jesus who appeared
first to Mary Magdalene
who sent her with the bursting
message
GO AND TELL...

I believe in the wholeness
of the Saviour
in whom there is neither
Jew nor Greek
slave nor free
male nor female
for we are all one
in salvation.

I believe in the Holy Spirit
as she moves over the waters
of creation
and over the earth.

I believe in the Holy Spirit
the women spirit of God
who like a hen
created us
and gave us birth
and covers us
with her wings.

*Rachel C. Wahlberg,
USA*

Credo

I believe in you, worker Christ light of light and true only begotten of God who to save the world in the humble and pure womb of Mary was incarnated.

I believe you were beaten, mocked and tortured, martyred on the cross while Pilate was praetor, the Roman imperialist, unscrupulous and soul-less, who by washing his hands wanted to erase the mistake.

I believe in you, friend, human Christ, worker Christ victor over death with the immense sacrifice, you engendered the new hope for liberation.

You are risen again in each arm that is raised to defend the people from the rule of the exploiter in the factory, in the school.

I believe in your struggle without truce. I believe in your resurrection.

**From
The Nicaraguan Campesino Mass,
by Carlos Jejia Godoy and
Pablo Martinez, NICARAGUA**

❖

From Jaini Bi — With Love [5]

Every noon at twelve
In the blazing heat
God comes to me
In the form of
Two hundred grams of gruel.

I know him in every grain
I taste him in every lick.
I commune with him as I gulp
For he keeps me alive, with
Two hundred grams of gruel.

I wait till next day noon
and now know he'd come;
I can hope to live one day more
For you made God to come to me as
Two hundred grams of gruel.

I know now that God loves me —
Not until you made it possible.
Now I know what you're speaking about
For God so loves this world
That he gives his beloved Son
Every noon through YOU.   INDIA

---

[5] *In 1973 Chitapur's famine-stricken people received substantial aid as a result of this poem, which was printed in magazines and newspapers throughout India and abroad.*

7

Go on our Way in Joy

Therefore, Go

God sends us into the world,
to accept the cost
and to discover the joy of discipleship.
Therefore go — carrying with you
the peace of Christ,
the love of God,
and the encouragement of the Holy Spirit,
in trial and rejoicing. Amen.

Ruth C. Duck, USA

The Blessing of the God of Sarah

The blessing of the God of Sarah and of Abraham,
the blessing of the Son, born of the woman Mary,
the blessing of the Holy Spirit who broods over us
as a mother with her children,
be with you all. Amen.

Lois Wilson, CANADA

45

Covenant with Me

Covenant with me
To spread community
To worlds beyond this place.

See afresh again
God's image in each one
Reflect that face ourselves.

Acknowledge human blur
Destruction, hurt, and sin
Confession brings forgiveness.

Sing anew God's praise
Accept our ministry
Begin the healing task.

Unite with those who love
Enough to move toward change
Empowered by the Spirit.

Go on our way in joy
Create a celebration
God's likeness lives in us!

Mary Freedlund, USA

No Longer Strangers

*Let us now depart
and hold fast to the Covenant,
knowing that in Christ we are
no longer strangers and sojourners
but dearly loved children
of the living God.*

Mary Sue Gast, USA

8

My Sisters Tell me...

Messengers

It suddenly strikes me
with overwhelming force:

It was women
who were first to spread the message of
Easter —
the unheard of!

It was women
who rushed to the disciples,
who, breathless and bewildered,
passed on the greatest message of all:

He is alive!

Think if women had kept silence
in the churches!

Märta Wilhelmsson, SWEDEN

It is with Shame

I am forty, or somewhere near, I'm told.
What I have learned is through my ears alone.
My eyes see only trees, the sky, my children, the food, my meagre wage.
In this way I am like all others—what is seen by them is seen by me—for all but one enormous thing—the words that people write and read.
These to me are but a bitter misery of mystery. When letters I must send, they are written by one child, ten, my son.
God knows if he writes it as I say, or some nonsense of his own.
My head was never schooled, only my hands, my back, my feet were trained to do the bidding of those who walk a higher path than me.
Deprived I was born, starved I will die, knowing nothing of any world but this, bounded by my unclean ignorance.
At the end of each stretch of thirty days, I take my pay and swear to it with one dirtied print of my right hand thumb.
Why this thumb is so different from any other will forever be my puzzle. It is with shame I press that paper, while those behind me laugh, for they take pen to hand and proudly sign a name for all to read.
Who can read a thumb? I vowed that never would my children live but half a life, and almost sooner than they walked I pushed them to a school.
There is no time now, at my old age, to learn to read what others tell, and content and passive I must remain, to see my sons rise somewhere near the sun.
I hope their skills will be reward enough, and when they walk their mighty road, they will take with them their mother in their hearts.

Margaret Duncan, INDIA

48

The Journey

I listen to the agony of God —
I who am fed,
who never yet went hungry for a day.
I see the dead —
the children starved for lack of bread —
I see and try to pray.

I listen to the agony of God —
I who am warm
who never yet lacked a sheltering home.
In dull alarm
the dispossessed of hut and farm
aimless and transient roam.

I listen to the agony of God —
I who am strong
with health and love and laughter in my soul.
I see a throng
of stunted children reared in wrong
and wish to make them whole.

I listen to the agony of God —
But know full well
That not until I share their bitter cry —
earth's pain and hell —
can God within my spirit dwell
to bring the Kingdom nigh.

I was hungry not just for food
    but for peace that comes from a pure heart.
I was thirsty not for water
    but for peace that satiates the passionate
    thirst for war.
I was naked not for clothes
    but for that beautiful dignity of men and
    women for their bodies.

I was homeless not for a shelter made of bricks
    but for a heart that understands, that covers,
    that loves.

I was hungry; I was thirsty; I was naked;
I was homeless.
    Yet I found peace, peace and dignity and
a heart that loves.

Nancy Telfer, CANADA

We Are Still Waiting

My sisters tell me
how people die of hunger
because there is no food to eat.

My sisters tell me
how people die of lack of hope
because they do not see a way out.

My sisters tell me
how people die of fear
submerged in silence, the silence of death.

My sisters tell me
how people die of sadness
because they have heaped treasures
and have lost their souls.

My sisters tell me
how people die of courage
because they have dared to speak up
to shout out against the oppressors.

Jesus Christ, the Son of God,
called the Prince of Peace
and (by mistake of the Roman authorities)
King of the Jews,
was executed
according to the fashion of the
occupant forces;
and died on the cross.
He had no army.
He had no resources.
He had no connections with the elite.
He did not turn stones into bread.
He did not establish the Kingdom.
He had no power.

My heart is trembling.
Couldn't He have turned those
stones into bread?
Couldn't He have jumped from
the temple walls?
Couldn't He have declared
Himself — ruler of the earth
and established the Kingdom?

Why those millions of bitter sighs?
Why those tears of anger?
Why those broken hopes and dreams?
Why that naked despair
   in the eyes of the little boy
   — my boy —
as he tried to escape the machine guns?

We are still waiting for the miracle.
The devil is still tempting us.

As if Christ were not risen,
As if the promise were not ours,
As if we could not have the courage to dare,
As if we had to be afraid,
As if the power of the Lord
were not present in our weakness.
We are still waiting for the miracle.

As if ...

Reinhild Traitler, AUSTRIA

❖

Mother[6]

If tomorrow, my mother,
Death should find me doubled
   over in a trench,
Don't weep.
The honour of your womb
Would then be my dead body.
My blood, the seed of new
   beginnings.
My life would then be a shout,
A flag symbolizing the
   struggle.

If tomorrow the enemy
Should place in your hands
My massacred body,
Don't weep.

Rather, be proud
That you gave our country
A son who would not be a slave,
Who preferred the silence
Of the centuries
To a moan produced
By the oppressor's lash.

"Madre",
Author unknown, NICARAGUA

---

[6] *This poem "Madre" was found stencilled on a wall in Leon, Nicaragua in 1979.*

First Tragedy

The yellow telegram
with its stark typewritten letters
announces a death
She knew it would be his death
still she mumbles the words
telling herself telling
herself don't cry
for this is common
in war who is ever free of tragedy

Just lie still lie still
You are free now my darling

Constantly thinking of the future
with a withering faith
she has painted her own portrait
the high collar the still-life round eyes
everything is black
because nothing is left
who has not suffered in a war

In confusion she looks down
at the seed coming to life in her
coming to the misery of life
try to grow up like your father my darling.

SOUTH VIETNAM

52

Who Am I

I am a woman
  I am Filipino[7]
    I am alive
      I am struggling
        I am hoping.

I am created in the image of God
just like all other people in the world;
I am a person with worth and dignity.
I am a thinking person, a feeling person,
  a doing person.
I am the small *I am* that stands before
  the big I AM.

I am a worker who is constantly challenged
  and faced with the needs of the church and
  society in Asia and in the global community.
I am angered by the structures and powers
  that create all forms of oppression, exploitation
  and degradation.
I am a witness to the moans, tears, banners and
  clenched fists of my people.
I can hear their liberating songs, their hopeful
  prayers and decisive march toward justice and
  freedom.

I believe that all of us — women and men
  young and old, Christians and all others —
  are called upon to do responsible action;
  to be concerned
  to be involved
  NOW!
I am hoping
  I am struggling
    I am alive
      I am Filipino
        I am a woman.

Elizabeth Tapia, THE PHILIPPINES

---

[7] *You may wish to change the nationality in this poem in order to adapt it to various contexts.*

Bakerwoman God

Bakerwoman God,
I am your living bread.
Strong, brown, Bakerwoman God,
I am your low, soft and being-
    shaped loaf.
I am your rising bread, well-kneaded
    by some divine and knotty pair of
    knuckles, by your warm earth-hands.
I am bread well-kneaded.

Put me in your fire, Bakerwoman God,
    put me in your own bright fire.

I am warm, warm as you from fire.
I am white and gold, soft and hard,
    brown and round.
I am so warm from fire.

Break me, Bakerwoman God.
I am broken under your caring Word.
Drop me in your special juice in pieces.
Drop me in your blood.
Drunken me in the great red flood.
Self-giving chalice, swallow me.
My skin shines in the divine wine.
My face is cup-covered and I drown.

I fall up in a red pool
    in a gold world
    where your warm sunskin hand is there
    to catch and hold me.
Bakerwoman God, remake me.

Alla Bozarth-Campbell, USA

9

God has Lifted up the Lowly

Mary and Martha

A reading based on Luke 10:38-42

While they were on their way Jesus came to a village where a woman named Martha made him welcome in her home. She had a sister, Mary, who seated herself at the Lord's feet and stayed there listening to his words. Now Martha was distracted by her many tasks, so she came to him and said: "Lord, do you not care that my sister has left me to get on with the work myself? Tell her to come and lend a hand". But the Lord answered: "Mary is listening to my message about freedom, and she has understood it as literally as it has to be understood. Therefore she remains sitting. Martha, you are fretting and fussing about so many things, because your world expects it from you as a woman, but I am not of this world. I bring freedom to the oppressed. Mary has received that freedom, do come and receive it too". And Martha tore her clothes and fell down at his feet and cried: "Lord, who is going to take care of the children and do the work?" But Jesus answered: "Let the children remain among us. Later on we will do the work together. You forget that those men who have understood the outreach of my gospel also have understood that freedom at the cost of women is not Christian freedom".

The Ecumenical Women's Group, Aarhus, DENMARK

Sarah and Hagar

Genesis 16 is a story about Sarah and Hagar, two women who are dependent upon the society which surrounds them. Their only duty in society is to fulfil the roles assigned to them as women within a patriarchal system—roles which make them competitors.

Genesis 16 describes a sequence of events. What effect have these events had on the lives of these two women?

What have they been feeling and thinking? Perhaps by putting ourselves in their situation we can learn what it means to be sisters.

The text is presented by three women: One, who reads the Biblical text, one who portrays Sarah's thoughts, and one who portrays Hagar's thoughts.

READER: **Genesis 16, 1a**
SARAH: I am Sarah. I am the wife of
Abram.
I am called Sarah,
Sarah, which means duchess.
But my name, my name has become
a disgrace for me.
I do not bear any children.
I am not at all capable of bearing a child,
I often think.
And I am distressed by this,
because I know what it implies.
I am the wife of Abram and that means
that I ought to take care
that this tribe, that this family
continues to exist.
It is not so important that I am here
it is important that the tribe goes on, the family,
and it is my duty and obligation
to give birth to children.
I am very distressed and I don't know
where I shall turn
with my despair.
Often I feel guilty and ask this God
why it is that I am not blessed
and am not fruitful.
Often I see my husband's looks
and then I feel myself under pressure.
In order that this family may persist, this tribe,
I will have to bear a child.

And I am growing older and older.
I am afraid that my husband, Abram,
will come to me one day and say
now I will take another wife
because you, Sarah, are not fruitful
I fear this degradation.
I see my maid Hagar.
Hagar is younger than I
and Hagar is beautiful.
I am considering what I can do.
Perhaps should I
before Abram decides
to take another wife in order to have sons,
ask Hagar
or suggest to Abram
that he take her, because she is the maid:
When she, the maid, bears a son,
then she still belongs to me
and therefore the child also belongs to me.
That I will do.
I will go to Abram.

READER: **Genesis 16:1b-2**
HAGAR: *I am Hagar, a maid from Egypt.*
For ten years already I have been away from Egypt.
At that time they led me away,
brought me to this foreign country.
I belong to the master and mistress,
I belong first to the mistress,
I am her chambermaid.
It is very hard in this country,
but I was very young when I had to leave home.
And it is miserable not to have any money,
to have been sold.
There is certainly a possibility
of finding a husband here,
perhaps one of the boy-servants.
But they are all different,
belonging to the other people,
I would also like to have children.
But there is no chance of that.
To live with the master and mistress
is—often—quite nice.
Sometimes I don't quite know what is wrong.
The mistress is becoming older
and often quite bitter.
The lord stares so strangely lately.
Often speaks quite politely to me.
And then she says
she soon wants to talk to me.
Something is in the making.

READER: **Genesis 16:3-4**

HAGAR: *I am Hagar and I am with child.*
So there was something in the making,
On the one hand it is absurd:
I am sent to a man
as if I were a piece of cattle
On the other hand: Abram is a nice man
and he is now more concerned about me.
I avoid the lady now.
She looks even more bitter.
But perhaps, perhaps it may even be a son
and that means I can stay here,
he will be the heir.
And then she can no longer exploit me.

SARAH: So that is the result:
because I am not fruitful,
because I am not with child,
I told my husband that he should take her.
And now that she is with child,
she makes herself important.
Now she is proud of her stupid stomach,
stands there, looking at me
as if I were her maid or something worse.
Makes it quite clear to me
what a piece of cattle I am,
and that I am worth nothing
because I have nothing in my womb.
My God, did this have to happen?
That which I wanted has happened,
and now, here is the bill.
She stands there looking down at me,
pointing out clearly what is of importance,
that it is not a question of
whether she is Hagar and I am Sarah,
but whether she has a child in her womb,
or even a son?
Oh, and how she shows it to me.
I am so distressed.
And now, when I see
how she suddenly looks at Abram...
I was hoping when I told Abram:
"take my maid,"
that she would still remain my maid
and not his wife in his thoughts.
But when I see her now
how she looks at my husband, Abram,
and when I see how Abram looks at her...

Not only does the child come through her,
but perhaps, perhaps he will actually
take her for his wife.
And I am the one to go my way
and stand there at the periphery.
I no longer know what to do.
For he is after all my husband.
I will go to Abram and talk to him...

READER: **Genesis 16:5-6a**
SARAH: I had at least hoped
that I could talk with my husband
about my situation.
I had hoped that Abram would have had
a bit of understanding for my feelings
a bit of understanding for me as a person,
that we could have talked about
what is now happening.
I had hoped.
But he, he says quite clearly
who I am for him,
that, what I feel doesn't count for anything.
What counts is what is in the stomach.
What counts is that I have the role of his wife
and that she has the role of my maid
it is that which counts.
Not how I am faring.
Ha, it is your matter,
what have I to do with Hagar he says.
Is she not your maid?
Before it was my matter to say:
"go and take her."
For him only the tribe is important.
Not to be able to talk with him
and Hagar who looks down on me...
There is only one chance of survival.
One single, simple, noble chance.
I am Sarah
and I am called duchess,
I will show her who is mistress here.
I must show her.

HAGAR: *Now again she appears as the lady.*
It is thus: I am dependent.
She is the mistress of the household
and she tries to master me.
She can try but the child still remains mine.

But I am afraid that she will take away the child from me
and then I will have to disappear.
But I know the way.
I came here from Egypt and I know the way back.
My name is Hagar, the fleeing.
There we are again:
to cut off is the only possibility.
And I will leave.
She will not get me,
nor will she get my child.

READER: **Genesis 16:6b.**

From
Sarah und Hagar
by
Heidemarie Langer
and Herta Leistner,
WEST GERMANY

Mary's Song
Luke 1:46-55

My heart praises the Lord;
my soul is glad because of
God my Savior,
for God has remembered me,
a lowly servant!
From now on all people
will call me happy,
because of the great things
the Mighty God has done for me.
God's name is holy;
from one generation to another
God shows mercy to those
who honor God.
God has stretched out a mighty arm
and scattered the proud
with all their plans.
God has brought down
mighty rulers from their thrones,
and lifted up the lowly.
God has filled the hungry
with good things
and sent the rich away
with empty hands.
God has kept the promise
God made to our ancestors
and has come to the help
of God's servant Israel.
God has remembered
to show mercy...

10

Called to Bear the Word

God of the Matriarchs

"I sent Moses to lead you, with... Miriam."

- **Prelude**

- **Call to Worship**

- **Hymn:**

- **Prayer of Confession**

Leader: If we claim to be sinless, we are self-deceived and strangers to the truth... and then his word has no place in us.

All: Hear us, O God, as we recall those who have sinned before us and, admitting ourselves to be in their lineage, attempt to become truthful before you.

   (Silence)

Leader: "But I have this against you, that you tolerate the woman Jezebel, who calls herself a prophetess and is teaching and beguiling my servants to practice immorality and to eat food sacrificed to idols." (Rev. 2:20)

All: We confess our forgetfulness, Lord, that you alone are God. We have followed after Jezebel, shameless lover of idols, worshiping other gods, exalting ourselves and our own dogmas at each other's expense. O God, claim our hearts once more.

* * *

Leader: "When Delilah saw that (Samson) had told her all his mind, she sent and called the lords of the Philistines, saying: 'Come up this once, for he has told me all his mind.' Then the lords of the Philistines came up to her, and brought the money in their hands.... Then she began to torment him, and his strength left him." (Judges 16:18,19)

All: We confess that we are often offspring of Delilah: eager to learn the secrets of others, we misuse our knowledge and bring them to ruin. God of truth, teach us to respect the truth.

* * *

Leader: "The sun had risen on the earth when Lot came to Zoar. Then the Lord rained on Sodom and Gomorrah brimstone and fire from the Lord out of heaven... But Lot's wife behind him looked back, and she became a pillar of salt." (Gen. 19:23-24, 26)

All: God of justice and mercy, we would not perish like the wife of Lot in our nearsighted clinging to the old and familiar. But we are woefully lacking in singleness of heart. Challenge us again.

* * *

Leader: "The scribes and the Pharisees brought a woman who had been caught in the act of adultery, and... they said to him, 'Teacher... in the law Moses commanded us to stone such. What do you say about her?'... But when they heard it, they went away, one by one... and Jesus said: 'Neither do I condemn you; go, and do not sin again.'" (John 8:3, 4, 9, 11)

All: Like the woman, may we, too, be surprised by the discovery of our true selves—new selves—in the light of your grace! Do not forget us, Lord: but lead us always nearer our heritages as your daughters and sons. In the name of Jesus Christ, let it be!

- **Assurance of Pardon**

- **Scripture: Luke 1:26-55**

- **Hymn:**

- **Meditation**

> **On Mary,** the mother of Jesus, who was deeply troubled over her strange new role, which the angel announced to her—that she was to be the bearer of the Word, the Saviour, the One who was to come to the throne of David. Mary asked the angel, "How can this be...?" His answer was that this was the work of the Holy Spirit and "with God nothing will be impossible". Henceforth Mary saw herself in a new way: "Behold, I am the handmaid of the Lord." It was a word of acceptance of the challenge and calling.
>
> We have also the eloquent song of Mary, the Magnificat, exclaiming in delight and affirmation, "He has regarded the low estate of his handmaiden." For in a world in which women were not even numbered among the human souls required to constitute a synagogue, in which women still counted as possessions of men, it was Mary—a woman—who was called to bear the Word. How little things have changed in two thousand years! Early in her calling, Mary recognized that God does indeed put down the mighty from their thrones and exalt those of low degree. Even at the time for her delivery, when the Word was to be revealed, Mary was turned away from the inn which should have received her. Nevertheless, she *did* give birth: the Word could not be turned aside or foiled, once it was spoken by God.
>
> And so it is, from beginning to beginning, that women were favoured first with the message of salvation. Mary was chosen to bear him figuratively—bodily; the women at the tomb bore the news verbally. They were commissioned, as we are, (no less than our husbands or male counterparts), to go quickly and tell: not primarily to arrange flowers or wash communion glasses, but in a multitude of creative and challenging ways, to enter the whole work of ministry!
>
> So there is hope for us. In spite of prejudice and hesitancy within the church, I cannot believe that the One who called us, be we women or men, will frustrate this purpose. Perhaps some future generation will call *us* blessed because we too were called to bear the Word. In the words of her kinswoman Elisabeth, as her own unborn child leaped for joy at the sound of Mary's voice, "Blessed is she who believed that there would be a fulfillment of what was spoken to her from the Lord!"

* * *

● **Litany of Praise and Hope**

> **Leader:** Let us not falter in hope! Let us offer our praise and our lives to the Lord.
>
> **Men:** God of the patriarchs...
>
> **Women:** God of the matriarchs...
>
> **All:** In line with all your faithful people in every age, we offer again ourselves and our gifts for the service of your kingdom!
>
> **Women:** God of Abraham, Isaac, and Jacob...
>
> **Men:** God of Sarah, Rebekah, and Rachel...
>
> **All:** Grant us the courage to cling to your promise, even if all the world seems hostile and our own hearts judge us failures.
>
> **Men:** God of Priscilla and Aquila...
>
> **Women:** God of Moses and of Miriam...
>
> **All:** May we too labour in harmony to bring our people out of bondage and darkness.
>
> **Women:** O God of Deborah, a mother in Israel, greatest of Israel's judges...
>
> **Men:** O God of Solomon, the wisest of kings...
>
> **All:** May our lives be but mirrors of your justice, lived out in the wisdom of unswerving faith.
>
> **Women:** Great God of Lydia, seller of purple...
>
> **Men:** Master of Paul, a maker of tents...
>
> **All:** Guide us into the world unafraid to lend our hands as well as our voices to your service, and eager to involve ourselves with all of your children.
>
> **Men:** And for the lives of all righteous women...
>
> **Women:** For past and present men of faith...
>
> **All:** For the ministries taking form within us, and for all the callings yet to be: The Lord's Name be Praised!

● **Benediction**

● **Postlude**

Gail Anderson Ricciuti, USA

66

Meditative Service on Images

This is a service of image-meditation on a given theme. Two (perhaps more) pictures (or slides) are exhibited beforehand in the room and illuminated. Quiet music should make it possible to focus in silence on the images.

The sequence of the service:

- **Introduction**
- **Greeting**
- **Hymn**
- **Reading of text**
- **Quietness — music**
- **Prayer or poem** — as a link between quietness and presentation of thoughts and reflections to others in the group.
- **Thoughts and reflections** — What new thoughts and insights came during the meditation? (Members of the group share their thoughts).
- **Prayer or poem**
- **Hymn**

EXAMPLE 1.

Women at the Cross, the Grave and the Resurrection

- **Images for meditation:** Two pictures: the women at the cross and the women at the resurrection.

- **Introduction:** The story has been handed down to us that women were present at the cross, that they went to the grave, and that they were the first to experience the resurrection. What significance does this story have in the tradition? What does it mean for us today?

- **Greeting:** We have set our hope on the living God, who is the Saviour of all humankind.

- **Hymn**

- **Reading of text:** Luke 23:26a, 27-28: "And as they led Jesus away a great multitude of the people... followed him, etc."
  John 19:25-27a
  Luke 23:52, 55-56: "Joseph of Arimathea, a member of the council, went to Pilate... etc."
  John 20:1 (instead of verse 2-10: She informs the disciples about the events—they all think it is theft).
  John 20:11-16.

- **Quietness — music**

- **Prayer or poem**

- **Thoughts and reflections**

- **Prayer or poem**

- **Hymn** (theme of resurrection)

EXAMPLE 2.

Bread

This pattern of worship could also be used with other themes, for example Christmas.
Around the theme "bread", an "agape" service can be made: Tables covered with white paper (or white sheets of paper fastened to the floor) with chairs (cushions) around.
On the tables: pencils and crayons with which to write and colour. A jar of wine or grapejuice, bread and pitchers.

- **Greeting**

- **Hymn**

- **Introduction**: What is bread? What comes to my mind when I think about bread? Let your mind wander for awhile. There are pencils and paper on the tables. Perhaps you can write down some associations, thoughts, sentences which come to you, without much conversation, but letting yourselves be inspired by each other in your thoughts.

- **Music**

- **Reading**: You can still let your thoughts wander, you can still write or close your eyes if you want to. I would like to say some things for your further reflection:

Bread:
Give us today our daily bread
no pie and no cake...

I don't bake the daily bread myself —
at the most I bake small buns from time to time...

I don't know how it is made any more-
to bake bread-sourdough-yeast-let the dough rise-
knead the whole mass...
I often go sour myself...
I can buy all sorts of bread
round, long, square — white, brown,
black — peasant — wood-oven baked,
full-grain, wheat...
BREAD
Others are without bread...

I live without bread, for the sake of my health
to remain slim
I must force myself to go hungry
I hunger for more...

Humankind does not live by bread alone...
what am I hungry for?
what do I live from?...

Jesus says: I am the bread of life ·
whoever comes to me will not hunger...

Give us today our daily bread...

About the friends of Jesus it is said:
They broke the bread together in their
homes...

Breaking the bread...

I share with somebody
I take part in the sharing.

Agape:

We have placed bread and juice here before you and
we would encourage you to share it with each other in
your small groups around the tables (sheets of paper).
Share also what is important for you, what is going on
within you, what is represented on your sheet of paper. Perhaps just leave a bit of time for being together.

Remain together, eating in the small groups for about
20 minutes while quiet music is played.

● **Prayer or poem**

● **Hymn**

*From
Frauen am Kreuz
am Grab bei der Auferstehung and
Brot und Rosen
by Heidemarie Langer
and Herta Leistner, WEST GERMANY*

Mary and Martha

The sketch which is part of this worship service is carried out by 3 women:

> The reader of the Biblical texts
> One woman to represent Mary
> One woman to represent Martha

Together the three shall clarify the text which is read and bring out the differences in the two personalities of Mary and Martha. The service is focused on the work in small groups and a Mary-Martha dialogue (debate) which follows after the group work.

THE SEQUENCE OF THE SERVICE:

- **Greeting and introduction**

- **Hymn**

- **Sketch:** The reading and dramatization of the scripture passage.

- **Group work:** The congregation is divided into two halves: one representing Martha, the other Mary. Within each half, work is done in subgroups of 3-4 persons. Each little group prepares 1-2 sentences within 5 minutes. These they will use later in the "Mary-Martha debate".

- **Plenary:** "Mary-Martha debate"
  The Marys and Marthas sit opposite each other in semi-circles and begin the debate. Participants from the two groups take turns in speaking: a Martha says 1-2 sentences, then a Mary answers with 1-2 sentences, etc.

- **Hymn**

EXAMPLE OF HOW A SERVICE CAN BE STRUCTURED

- **Introduction:** Through tradition we have learned that Mary is better than Martha. We have been struck by this since most of us do not escape Martha's duties in the home. We feel that the story of Luke 10, 38-42 is a good starting point for examining questions such as: two women and Jesus, how to be a disciple, ways of relating to God and Jesus, how to be sisters, relating to one another.

- **Hymn**

- **Sketch:** Reader stands in front of the group.
  Mary sits on the floor not far from the reader.
  Martha is outside at the beginning.

Martha:	(running into the room): "Mary, Mary, Jesus is here! As usual with his whole group of followers, and I have invited them to our house. We will have to prepare something to eat quickly. Do we still have something in the freezer?" (goes ahead into the kitchen). "Always these twelve along with him; I am glad but how will I manage?" (moves excitedly about the kitchen).
Reader:	Luke 10:38-39. (read "Jesus" instead of "him" in verse 38).
Martha:	(from the kitchen): "Do you know where the salt is Mary?"

Pause

Reader:	Luke 10:40a.
Martha:	(coming in): Luke 10:40b (read "Jesus" instead of "Lord"). Possibly restate in spoken language form.
Reader:	Luke 10:41-42, (read "Jesus" instead of "the Lord" in verse 41).
Reader:	(leaves). Mary and Martha are alone.
Martha:	Now he is again gone with his disciples... I'm still quite good at cooking if I may say so.
Mary:	Yes, I think there were some... Yes, perhaps we should talk about it...
Martha:	Yes, but I cannot talk with you now. I must be a moment on my own and reflect a bit...

Mary:	Yes, I think that is sensible, because, if we clash now... so let us talk together later, when we find some time...
Mary:	(to her half of the group): I would like to think with you on what we can say later on in the talk with Martha...
Martha:	(to her half of the group): And I would like to think with you on what we will say to Mary later...

- **Group work**

- **Plenary:** Some examples of what women have said in a "Mary-Martha debate":

Martha:	Mary, I find that it was very unfair.
Mary:	Martha, I think it was good that somebody finally appealed to your reason.
Martha:	And what if everybody only just listens? I would like to have that experience, so that next time I'll listen too and everyone will have to take care of their own hunger, arriving tired after the journey...
Mary:	Actually I had a very bad feeling sitting there and not doing anything, because I too feel that it's nice when we eat together...
Martha:	I had been looking forward to it and wanted to prepare something good, I wanted to express my joy. I was only cross because I wanted to do both. I wanted us to have something to eat so that we would enjoy ourselves at the common meal. But I also wanted to listen. If I hadn't wanted that too I wouldn't have become so cross...
Mary:	I find that we're actually both rather stupid because we didn't think of the possibility that the men could also have helped in the kitchen... I think it is important that we consider such things in advance...
Martha:	Yes, let us in future prepare and act together...

- **Hymn**

From
Maria und Martha
by Heidemarie Langer
and Herta Leistner, WEST GERMANY

A Workshop Worship

This is a description of a workshop worship where the participation of all those present is especially accented. It can be used at conferences and with special groups of people, but also as a parish worship.
The worship which is described here took place on a Sunday afternoon in a parish church.

We knew before we came to the worship service that it would take longer than a usual worship. We had been told that it would probably last two to three hours.

The service started with singing together and then the leader gave an introduction. She told us that this was a service where we would all participate and contribute in different ways. Some of us would work in a group on preparing a message or a short sermon; others would prepare a large painting to hang in front of the church. Others would prepare prayers and others a confession of sins. Still others would prepare a confession of faith. Some people would write poems, some would bake the bread for the Eucharist, some would make up a pantomime on the theme. There was a choir and a music group who had prepared some music in advance and those who wanted to practice singing and learning the songs were able to stay with them.

The leader told us who would be in charge of each of the groups and also that we could choose in which preparatory group we wanted to participate.

The leader then gave a brief outline of the theme of the worship service and read a Bible text on the theme.

Then came the group work. The different groups spread out in the whole church. In every corner there were people actively preparing the different parts of the service.

There were some people who for a number of reasons did not want to join a group They were not allowed to wander around looking at the work of the others, but were given something to read by themselves on the theme.

After about 30-40 minutes of group work, everyone gathered together.

The leader hung up a large sheet of paper (1 X 2 meters), where she had written down the order in which the worship would continue. The songs, confessions, prayers, sermon, text reading, pantomime, presentation of the painting, were all included. It was good to have the order visible like this because in that way all the groups knew when it was their turn. Of course the leader also told each group when it was their turn.

It was amazing how the people could make such rich contributions in such a short time. The music was strong and happy, the prayers closely related to people's lives, the confessions engaging and the poems thoughtful. The fascinating painting surprised us. Many people said after

74

the service how important it had been to them to be able to contribute concretely. They felt that the service had been very much their own worship, rather than a performance by a few people for "the many". It had been an event where they felt at home and where their own presence was important. And isn't that what worship services should all be?

Instructions to the leader:

Before the worship: *Meet with the co-workers and choose a theme and a Bible text, prepare material for group work, arrange for a music group, choir or other music leader to come. And remember when you advertise the worship that it will take two to three hours.*

Some possible tasks for the groups on the given theme:
- *Preparing the sermon/reflections.*
- *Painting a wall painting and/or in other ways prepare the room, flowers, candles, etc.*
- *Baking bread for the Eucharist.*
- *Formulating prayers.*
- *Preparing a dance — for all to participate in, or as their own expression on the theme.*
- *Writing poems.*
- *Group making music.*
- *Formulating or choosing a confession — of sin and/or faith.*
- *Making sculptures of simple material.*
- *Any other task in connection with the worship.*

Christina Lövestam, SWEDEN

BIBLIOGRAPHY

Abayasekera, Jeffrey and Niles, D. Preman, eds.
For the Dawning of the New,
The Commission on Theological Concerns, The Christian Conference of Asia,
Singapore, 1981.

Amundsen, Sandy and Moriarty, Irene, eds.,
Woman-Soul Flowing: Words for Personal and Communal Reflection,
Ecumenical Women's Center, Chicago, 1978.

Althouse, La Vonne and Srook, Lois K.,
In God's Image: Towards Wholeness for Women and Men,
Division for Mission in No. America, Lutheran Church of America, 1976.

Bardh, Ulla; Billinger, Kerstin; Byström Janarv, Görel; Lindqvist,
Kerstin and Olsson, Lena, eds.
Halva himlen är vår (Half the Heaven is Ours).
Verbum Förlag A.B., Älvsjö, Sweden, 1979.

Bardh, Ulla; Lundberg, Lars Åke and Olsson, Lena, eds.
Öppna Din Mun… Kvinnor predikar (Open Your Mouth… Women Preaching).
Skeab Truckmans, Stockholm, 1981.

Bausch, Michael G. and Duck, Ruth C., eds.,
Everflowing Streams: Songs for Worship,
The Pilgrim Press, New York, 1981.

Because We Are One People,
Ecumenical Women's Center, Chicago, 1974.

Bozarth-Campbell, Alla,
Womanpriest, A Personal Odyssey,
Paulist Press, New Jersey, 1978.

— Gynergy,
Wisdom House Press, Minneapolis, 1978.

Christ, Carol P. and Plaskow, Judith, eds.,
Womanspirit Rising: A Feminist Reader in Religion,
Harper and Row, San Francisco, 1979.

Church of Sweden Mission,
Amandla: Kamp-och lovsang från Sydafrika,
Svenska Kyrkens Mission, Sweden,

Clark, Linda; Ronan, Marian and Walker, Eleanor,
Image-Breaking/Image-Building: A Handbook for Creative Worship
with Women of Christian Tradition,
The Pilgrim Press, New York, 1981.

The Community of Women and Men in the Church: Report of the Asian Consultation,
Bangalore, 1978.
Sponsored by the World Council of Churches, Commission on Faith,
and Order, Geneva.

Duck, Ruth C., ed.,
Bread for the Journey: Resources for Worship,
The Pilgrim Press, New York, 1981.

Grana, Janice, compiler,
Images: Women in Transition,
The Upper Room, Nashville, Tennessee, 1976.

International Review of Mission, Vol. 71, No. 282, April 1982.
World Council of Churches, Geneva.

Kahl, Susanne; Langer, Heidemarie; Leistner, Herta and Moltmann-Wendel, Elisa-
beth,
Feministische Theologie-Praxis Arbeitshilfen, 3,
Evangelische Akademie. Bad Boll, W. Germany, 1981.

Neufer Emswiler, Sharon and Tom,
Sisters and Brothers Sing,
Wesley Foundation Campus Ministry, Normal, Illinois.

— Women and Worship: A Guide to Non-Sexist Hymns, Prayers and Liturgies,
Harper and Row, New York, 1974.

Nguyen Ngoc Bich, translator,
A Thousand Years of Vietnamese Poetry,
Alfred A. Knopf, New York, 1975.

O'Grady, Alison, ed.,
Voices of Worship: An Asian Anthology, Volumes I and II,
Asian Church Women's Conference, Seoul, Korea, 1982.

Sing a Womansong,
Ecumenical Women's Center, Chicago.

Something About Women in Danish Churches,
The Ecumenical Women's Group, Aarhus, Denmark, 1980.

Swidler, Arlene, ed.,
Sistercelebrations,
Fortress Press, Philadelphia, 1974.

"Tell Out Tell Out My Glory", Risk, Vol. 9, No. 3, 1973
World Council of Churches, Geneva.

Wahlberg, Rachel Conrad,
Jesus According to a Woman,
The Missionary Society of St. Paul the Apostle, New York, 1975.

Jesus and the Freed Woman,
Paulist Press, New Jersey, 1978.

Watkins, Keith,
Faithful and Fair: Transcending Sexist Language in Worship,
Abingdon Press, Nashville, Tennessee, 1981.

Women and Men in Asia: The Woman Question in the Asian Context.
Part One, WSCF Asia Women's Workshop, Bangalore, 1976,
World Student Christian Federation Asia Regional Office, Hong Kong, Book No. 5,
1977.

ACKNOWLEDGEMENTS

Concerning Copyrights: We have attempted to acquire permission for all the pieces included in this book that are not in the public domain. If we have overlooked anyone, we apologize and would appreciate having the omission brought to our attention. Thank you.

Page 23: ''A Litany of Thanks'' by Willa Roghair, in *Woman-Soul Flowing: Words for Personal and Communal Reflection,* eds., Sandy Amundsen and Irene Moriarty. Ecumenical Women's Center, Chicago, 1978.

Page 25: ''O God of a Thousand Names and Faces'' by Sharon Owens, in *Image-Breaking/Image-Building,* by L. Clark, M. Ronan, E. Walker. Pilgrim Press, 1981. P. 60f. Used by permission.

Page 27: ''O God What has thou to say?'' by P. Mookan, in *For the Dawning of the New,* eds., Jeffrey Abayasakera and D. Preman Niles. The Christian Conference of Asia, Singapore, 1981.

Page 28: ''I Cry in the Night from the Torture Chamber, Psalm 129.'' (Clamo En la Noche En La Camara de Tortura, Salmo 129), by Ernesto Cardenal. Translated from the Shamish. Carlos Lohlé S.A., Buenos Aires. © Used by permission.

Page 34: ''Lord Remind Me'' in *International Review of Mission,* Vol. 71, No. 282, April 1982, WCC. Used by permission.

Page 40: ''I Believe'' by Norma, in *Magdalena* magazine, December 1981, Australia. Used by permission.

Page 46: ''Covenant With Me'' by Mary Freelund in Concern Magazine, November 1979. Used by permission of United Presbyterian Women.

Page 48: ''Saraswati'' (Goddess of Learning), by Margaret Duncan, YWCA of India, New Dehli. Used by permission.

Page 49: ''The Journey'' by Nancy Telfer, reprinted with permission from G.V. Thompson, Ltd., Toronto, Canada, 1982 ©.

Page 54: ''Baker Woman God'' by Alla Bozarth-Campbell from *Gynergy,* Wisdom House Press, Minneapolis, 1978. Used by permission.

Page 63: ''God of the Matriarchs'' was adapted for inclusive language and used by permission of Fortress Press.

Page 67: Feministiche Theologie-Praxis, Ein Werkstattbuch, *Arbeitshilfen,* No. 3, May, 1981. Evangelische Akademie, Bad Boll, West Germany. Used by permission.

Photo credits: ISIS, pp. 8, 26, 41; WSCF, pp. 20, Lucia Vernerelli, 42, 48 and 52; Kirkernes Raceprogram, Denmark, p. 28; Kathe Kollwitz, p. 37; Aurelia da Silva, p. 60.